T0164905

INSIGHTS INTO THE DESIGN OF LIFE

# KARMA SUTRA

## LAMA LAMI

Foreword by Suma Varughese, Editor, Life Positive Magazine

**BALBOA.**
PRESS

A DIVISION OF HAY HOUSE

Balboa Press books may be ordered through booksellers or by contacting:

Balboa Press
A Division of Hay House
1663 Liberty Drive
Bloomington, IN 47403
www.balboapress.com.au
1-(877) 407-4847

ISBN: 978-1-4525-0380-6 (sc)
ISBN: 978-1-4525-0381-3 (e)

Because of the dynamic nature of the Internet, any web addresses or
links contained in this book may have changed since publication and
may no longer be valid. The views expressed in this work are solely those
of the author and do not necessarily reflect the views of the publisher,
and the publisher hereby disclaims any responsibility for them.

The author of this book does not dispense medical advice or prescribe the use
of any technique as a form of treatment for physical, emotional, or medical
problems without the advice of a physician, either directly or indirectly. The
intent of the author is only to offer information of a general nature to help
you in your quest for emotional and spiritual well-being. In the event you use
any of the information in this book for yourself, which is your constitutional
right, the author and the publisher assume no responsibility for your actions.

Any people depicted in stock imagery provided by Thinkstock are models,
and such images are being used for illustrative purposes only.
Certain stock imagery © Thinkstock.

Printed in the United States of America

Balboa Press rev. date: 02/18/2012

*For Aarav, Krish, Sahil, Smriti and Samir*

Life can only be understood backwards, but it must be lived forwards.

—Kierkegaard

# Contents

## Insights

## Stories

# Resources

*Life doesn't come with an Operating Manual—we put it together the best we can and then bumble our way through it. Late in life, we begin to get the hang of it by which time we have already made all our mistakes and often a clumsy hash of it. Hindsight wisdom is of limited use and the youngsters who are at the threshold of life are no takers for hand-me-down wisdom because they want to come to their own conclusions through their own experience, and rightly so. Still, here is a list of work that opened my mind to fresh perspectives and made me investigate the automatic, unquestioned way of being as the only way to be. Each one of these proved to be a quantum leap in my slow and arduous journey to make sense of life and showed me that there are always choices.*

*The Road Less Travelled by M. Scott Peck*
*Landmark Forum*
*Enneagram*
*I'm OK, You're OK by Thomas A. Harris*
*Games People Play by Eric Berne*
*Man's Search for Meaning by Viktor Frankl*
*The Bhagvad Gita—a Hindu scripture*
*Power of Now by Eckhart Tolle*
*A New Earth by Eckhart Tolle*
*Vipassna Meditation*
*Thousand Names for Joy by Byron Katie*

*Loving What is by Byron Katie*
*Byron Katie's The Work*
*Multiple Intelligences by Howard Gardner*
*What the Bleep do we Know?*
*What the bleep!? Down the Rabbit hole*

# A Lama without a Monastic Order

*My close ones call me Lami—abbreviated from the second half of my first name—Neelam. After my hair-loss due to chemotherapy, people would often comment that I looked like a Lama. The alliteration was irresistible and so I became Lama Lami—a self-initiated Lama without a monastic order or robes. My unofficial initiation into lama-hood is also owed to an experience of Satori which the cancer episode left me with. Much has been said and written about living in denial of mortality but really, there is something to be said for living in the face of it. Present moment awareness is a practice I had been labouring at for a long time. But the mind, with its tendency to constantly wander away to memories of the past or anticipation of the future, is hard to hold on to. I started using the constant thought of mortality as a peg to tether my mind to stay 'here and now'. That helped me deal mindfully with a cancer that has since relapsed four times in as many years. I learnt that I undergo stress, anxiety or a sense of calamity only when I either connect with a past experience or anticipate a future event. For instance, I might feel anxious when I recall what my mother went through when she was battling cancer. Or, I might worry about having to go through painful chemotherapy all over again, every time I relapse. In each case, I am either in the past (memory of mother's suffering) or in the future (anticipating pain). I then 'suffer' vicariously, even though there is no pain or discomfort in the body at that moment. This is the kind of suffering that practicing the power of now has helped me overcome. Whenever the mind veers towards fear of what might befall me, I bring myself back to the present moment, knowing that I can deal with whatever comes up, only when it comes up.*

*What helps me when I am in the moment of actual physical pain is the profound realization of the Buddhist saying: 'pain is inevitable but suffering is an option'. I consciously limit the experience of pain to a sensation in the body and not add mental suffering to it by feeling unfortunate, resisting the pain or wishing it away. Surrendering to the reality of the moment is my mantra for the end of suffering.*

*In the preceding years I had been 'on the path' for quite some time and the carrot that had kept me going was the lure of a halo! During the early years, I actually wore an imaginary one round my head. As someone with spiritual inclinations and a few insights, I had a holier-than-thou chip on my shoulder. But as the practice of present moment awareness deepened my insights, the chip fell off and the halo evaporated. I realized— with some disappointment, I will admit, that there is no halo at the end of the spiritual rainbow; that the rainbow is its own reward.*

*I recall a moment of epiphany long before my engagement with spirituality. I was on the rooftop of a high-rise—shooting the cityscape for a corporate film. During an idle moment, I was observing the crisscrossing streets below and the toy-like vehicles purposefully navigating the roads. One stretch of the street was choked with traffic and from that height I could clearly see that the cars headed for it could easily by-pass the jam by making a right, then left on a parallel road and then left again to meet the same road up ahead; and actually get there faster, than by taking the straight road. But the drivers on the ground couldn't see that and they all continued on their pre-determined path, getting caught in the traffic jam ahead.*

*I was struck by the thought of how an over-arching view can clarify the course. The sweeping perspective at my command gave me a clear view of the future course of that traffic and the alternative courses. Spirituality gives us that over-arching vantage where we can see ground-reality in a larger totality and see that there is not just one pre-determined course—there are always choices. It helps us transcend the constrained reality of our limited experience and tune in to a higher intelligence. Life can then be navigated with far more clarity without running into roadblocks.*

*For the longest time, I berated myself for my need to wrap my head around existential and spiritual concepts rather than experiencing spirituality. Gradually, I dropped my resistance to my need to understand—because understanding, I realized, is my portal to realization. When one is on the path of seeking, all roads lead to realization of spiritual lessons. Everything assumes a koan-like quality—a chance remark here, an anecdote there can lead to an epiphany. Through Karma Sutra, I share motley stories, insights and revelations about life as we see it and as we don't.*

*The stories included here carry the essence of spiritual teachings. Culled from various wisdom traditions, some may be familiar, yet may make a point you had earlier missed. A picture, they say, is worth a thousand words. It has a tremendous recall value because the mind retains visuals better than thoughts. A story is worth a thousand pictures because it evokes mental pictures as we read, that get retained in our memory like a comic book or a* storyboard. Stories are a useful tool on the spiritual path because when we begin to walk the talk and start practicing what we learn, we tend to waver. We regress to our old, habitual way of living life—and that is when we need a timely reminder. A story has a way of coming to mind at just such a time, to set us back on track.

To share from personal experience, I heard the one titled 'Enough' around the time I needed to hear it most. My husband, barely into his forties, had suddenly died of cardiac arrest without any warning or previous history. Apart from coping with the tragedy, the mantle of bread-winner to a family of four—me, my two children and my mother-in-law—sat very heavy on my shoulders. Although I was running a successful advertising business at that time, anxiety attacks would grip me in the middle of the night leaving me in a hell of panic. I would try to work through those anxiety attacks with every tool in my New Age kit—deep breathing, mind control, affirmations—but none of these would hold up to the intensity of the attack. And then invariably, this story, which is about abundance being a state of mind rather than a state of finances, would pop up in my head—and give me so much solace that I would go back to sleep.

I hope this book makes a good travel companion on your journey.

*Godspeed!*
*Lama Lami*

# Foreword

Neelam is a very dear friend. We met a few years ago at one of the annual Expos the magazine I edit, Life Positive, holds in New Delhi. Boldly, Neelam came up to me and told me I was her soul mate.

It turned out that she was right. She moved to Mumbai soon after because of her prolonged engagement with cancer and she actually settled down a 10-minute walk from my house. To have a close friend as a neighbour is an unbelievable blessing and Neelam and I have made the most of it— getting together as often as we can for cozy lunches and teas, and always for stimulating conversation.

So I know Neelam and I can testify that the insights she offers in this brief but potent book have been soldered in the furnace of her life.

Ever since I have known her, Neelam has been battling cancer and I have never met a more valiant or intrepid warrior. She has had many remissions and each time, with an almost nonchalant poise, Neelam has shown up for yet another joust with the beast. Chemotherapy has became pretty much a constant, but how lightly she has worn this ominous and agonizing presence. In fact, if I had a grouse against her it was that she simply was never around. One day she would be home resting with chemo and the next I heard from her was that she was holidaying in Dubai or Delhi or even Kerala. In between she found the time to dispose of all her property in Delhi and simply and lightly take roost in Mumbai. I watched her buy a flat, decorate it beautifully with her classic good taste, buy and sell a shop, buy a car and a hundred other ventures which would have given me nightmares without even turning a hair.

But what is truly awe-inspiring is that I have never to date heard her whinge or grouse about the pain and discomfort she is going through. Even as I write this, cancer is causing her more than grave discomfort yet it is possible to discuss spirituality, exchange jokes and even have her sympathetically listen to my own grouses about life.

There is almost no one I know who symbolises grace under pressure more than Neelam. In the essays and short stories that follow, Neelam shares with us the source of her strength and serenity—the constant practice of being in the Now. The recognition that pain is inevitable but suffering is optional has enabled her to whittle down the situation to its bare bones and discard the peripherals—the drone of thoughts, complaints, fantasies, resistances and so on that is the mark of the mind.

"One of the most valuable insights I have had ever since I set out on the path of self-inquiry is that I don't live in the world—I live inside a story," she observes with acuity. Each of us is indeed locked into a unique world composed of our likes, dislikes, perceptions, judgements, experiences and unique vision. And it is this story that we need to break out of in order to see life as it is, the moment as it is, the situation as it is.

Neelam has the unique gift of following the trajectory of a thought to its logical conclusion—chasing the thought to its lair so to speak. In the process she helps unveil the many illusions that stop us from perceiving what she calls the 'design' of life.

Each essay is thought-provoking; its relentless pursuit of the truth admirable and its insights inspiring.

There is much to learn from Karma Sutra as I have discovered to my delight.

Suma Varughese

# Hymn of Creation

Then even non-existence was not, nor existence.
There was no atmosphere then, nor the heavens beyond it.
What concealed it? Where was it? In whose keeping?
Was there then cosmic water, in unfathomed abyss?

Then there were neither death nor immortality,
Nor was there then the distinction of night and day.
The One breathed windlessly by its own power.
There was that One then, and there was no other.

Darkness was hidden by darkness.
All was an undistinguishable sea.
That One which came to be, enveloped in void,
That Alone was born of the power of heat.

Upon that desire descended in the beginning—
That was the seed thought, born of the mind.
The sages have searched their hearts with wisdom
To discover this to be what links the existent to the non-
existent.

And they have stretched their cord across the void,
And know what was above, and what below,
Seminal powers made fertile mighty forces.
Inherent power below; impulses above

But, after all, who knows, and who can say
Whence it all arose, and whence this creation?
The gods themselves are subsequent to this creation,
So who knows truly whence it has arisen?

Whence all creation has come into being,
He, whether he created it or not,
He, who surveys it all from highest heaven,
Surely he knows—or perhaps even he knows not.

Rig Veda

"We don't see things as they are; we see them as we are."

—*Anais Nin*

# Life as we 'Know' it

In a village far, far away lived a man who was quite unhappy. He was a very righteous man who lived by a set code of conduct. He really believed very strongly in his code of morality and wished that everybody else would live from it too. But not everybody around him felt the same way and as a result, he was always at odds with them. He was always irritated and annoyed with the villagers for this reason. Finally, one day he decided that he was sick and tired of arguments and disagreements. "I think it would be a good idea to quit this village and move to another where I can live amidst like-minded people," he thought. So he packed up his belongings, loaded his cart and off he rode in search of a new village.

As he approached the gates of a new village, he was filled with doubts and misgivings about the kind of people he would find in the new village. Just then, a village elder came out of the village gate. So he called out to the old man, "Pray sire, what kind of people dwell in this village?" The old man looked at the traveller and his cart loaded with his belongings and asked, "What kind of people dwelt in the village you come from?"

"Oh! Don't ask!" replied the traveller, "the people back where I come from have no sense of right and wrong; they are very annoying, quarrelsome and ignorant. But alas! They are not ready to learn so you can't teach them anything."

"How unfortunate!" said the old man, "For so you shall find them here!"

Disappointed, the traveller carried on in search of another village.

A little later another traveller rode up with all his belongings in the cart and encountered the same wise man.

"Pray sire," he asked, "what kind of people dwell in this village? I am a trader in search of new markets and so I need to keep moving to new places."

Again, the old man asked, "What kind dwelt in the village you come from?"

"Oh! They were good people—friendly, trusting and very cooperative—all in all, a good lot!"

"What a coincidence!" replied the wise man, "for so you shall find them here."

## Insight

1.  Our opinions are a dead give-away of who we are.
2.  The outer world is a shadow of our inner world.
3.  Our self is constantly reflected in our circumstances.

4. We project our experience onto the world and then feel surprised at the repetitive pattern of the way it occurs to us no matter where we go.

5. We humans live inside a story which shows up in our description of reality.

# The Design of 'I'

*'I' am a story—the story of everyman and everywoman. This is the story of how we come to be who we come to be.*

One of the most valuable insights I have had ever since I set out on the path of self-inquiry is that I don't live in the world—I live inside a story. Like Alice, I fell down a rabbit hole sometime early in life and landed in a wonderland—a fictional fantasy of my own making. The story I live inside is not the story of *my life*, it is *my story* of life, my unique perspective and my interpretation of the world as I experienced it from birth until now. In here, I see the world not as it is but as it occurs to me.

What I think of as my life is actually just a story I have about it. I am the unacknowledged author of a story I call 'my life'. I have been cribbing and complaining about the rotten script all along and to think that the story has been scripted by none other than me. It has 'me' writ large all over it. When I utter the word 'world', I think I am talking about the same thing that you call the world. But my perspective and understanding of it is as unique as yours and therefore the two are distinctly different. There is no world out there— there is your version of it and there is my version of it; your interpretation of it and my interpretation of it; there is your world and there is my world. Planet earth is inhabited by 7 billion worlds for each one of us lives cocooned in the world of our story.

The story that we run has a tremendous significance because the story then runs our life. The story is our unconscious creation. It is a series of meanings and interpretations that we unwittingly attributed to events early on. We repeatedly interpreted events in our own unique way, filtered through an emotional bias. These biases then started showing up as recurrent patterns. These patterns, in turn, started showing up as our personality with all our emotional overtones, our strengths and our weaknesses. Seeking out what made us feel good and avoiding what made us uncomfortable became our religion. What we sought came in different shapes and forms—it could be appreciation, affection, admiration, being followed or being feared—because it made us feel powerful. Then we learnt to make connections about what got others to make us feel good and what didn't. We started repeating what got others to treat us the way we wanted to be treated and avoiding what got them to say what we didn't want to hear. The bouquets and brickbats decided for us, what to become. We were little kids trying to cope in an adult world. The world occurred to us as an asymmetrical place where the adults were in control of our life and seemed to know what they were talking about. It is only much later, when we become adults that we realize that they were just as clueless, confused and vulnerable.

Up until then, we were human-beings, now we turned into human-becomings. We developed a good sense of self about the parts of us that worked well—these became our winning formulas. Slowly, we began to construct a picture of our 'self' from all this. Despite the confusion and contradictions, a pattern began to emerge and our personality began to form. Depending on what got us to feel good we either became driven to achieve or easy-going; aggressive or submissive; serious or funny, a bully or a victim. We chose one or the other on the basis of what we enjoyed being thought of. Ever since, we have been preoccupied with our image more than our real self—what others thought of us became more important than who we actually are. We started getting defined by opinions. We have been trying since to—look a little more beautiful by donning makeup; appear a little more affluent with acquisitions; sound a little more intelligent or powerful . . . We painted a face that we wanted the world to see and wore it like a mask, hoping the world would never get to see the real one behind it. Our movement from being to becoming was a movement from a state of harmony to a state of constant toil and endeavour in order to fit in. This constant need for acknowledgment became an addiction. If we thought being feared got us admiration, we started playing power games; If we felt we were in people's way when we needed help, we became meek and self-effacing; if our accomplishments got appreciated, we became driven to achieve; and if, on the other hand, we thought pleasing others got us approval, we became compliant and so on and so forth. The need for approval and the fear of disapproval drove our every action. We have been conditioned by injunctions and permissions such that all there is to us is an interwoven mesh of approval and disapproval. Like the invisible man, we are the clothing of conditioning with no me inside. This realization is the beginning of our search for the missing self. We never came into our own even when we grew up. Perhaps because there was no watershed event called 'growing up'—it just kept happening a day at a time. So we just kept following the same pattern of seeking love in its many variants—approval, appreciation, admiration, being followed or being feared. We grew up embracing certain parts of us and disowning certain other parts. It is because of these disavowed parts that we no longer feel whole and complete. We keep thinking that one person's unconditional love, or the admiration of many, or the acquisition of wealth or maybe knowledge, will enhance us to wholeness.

If we look long and hard, we can see how we came to be who we came to be. Our story is a valuable source of self knowledge; it is a storehouse of information about our strengths, blind spots and challenges. It is a map that shows us where we are located and the way leading to various alternative futures from there. The map can help us chart our course afresh, to the desired future and we can be the conscious creator of our destiny. How we came to have certain biases which then went on to make up our unique personality is not important, what is important is to get a complete understanding of how they impact us. A story once begun has a foregone conclusion—a bit like the role of destiny in Greek tragedy. If we allow it to stay in the domain of the unconscious, we are destined to helplessly play out the script, without any choice in the matter. If, on the other hand, we begin to see that it is we who chose the biases that we chose, albeit unconsciously, we begin to own authorship of the story. By owning the authorship, we gain control over the script. This is the beginning of power. The hold of destiny is loosened and instead of playing out the story we begin to make conscious choices and take our life in the desired direction.

*My first eye-opener on the path was the understanding that we all are strait-jacketed in a mould which is our personality type and that our personality is what we need freedom from in order to respond to a situation creatively and not automatically or repetitively. Not only did this give me an insight into my own inner machinations but an understanding that others too are acting out of their own personality traps. I got this insight from an Enneagram workshop conducted by Luiz Carlos a brilliant Brazilian gentleman whose grip on the subject was complete. The Enneagram is derived from South American wisdom tradition and was later used extensively by Gurdjieff in his teachings. According to Wikipedia, "The Enneagram of Personality is . . . a typology that . . . has been widely promoted in both business management and spiritual contexts through seminars, conferences, books, magazines and DVDs. In business contexts it is generally used as a typology to gain insights into workplace dynamics; in spirituality it is more commonly presented as a path to higher states of being, essence and enlightenment. It has been described as a method for self-understanding and self-development but has been criticized as being subject to interpretation, making it difficult to test or validate scientifically."*

"Out beyond ideas of wrongdoing and right-doing there is a field. I will meet you there. When the soul lies down in that grass, the world is too full to talk about."

—Rumi

# Where to Look

Late one night, a man was walking down a dark alley. Up ahead, he saw another man frantically looking for something under a lamp post. The man walked up to him and asked, "Can I help?"

"Thanks!" said the second man. "I dropped a precious coin and I just can't seem to find it."

The first man joined the hunt. Both men looked and looked but no coin showed up on the street. "Where the hell did you drop it?" asked the first man exasperated.

"Over there, by the curb-side at the far end of the street," said the second man.

"Then why the hell are we looking here, under the lamp post?" yelled the first man.

"Because it is completely dark over there!"

## Insight

1.  Divinity is whole and complete.
2.  In order to find our wholeness and completeness we need to look in the dark recesses marked 'guilt'

and 'shame' where we dropped certain parts of our precious 'self'.

3. We keep looking for it in the lit up part—our conscious mind.

4. We need to embrace our so-called darkness to be whole and complete.

rules except that morality has got sanctified by religion and comes with an enormous baggage. We don't identify our 'character,' for instance, with observance of traffic rules but we have internalised morality such that it has become the voice of what we call our 'conscience'. We have (con)fused morality with who we are. The reason is that we no longer see it as a man-made code of conduct but as a divinely ordained code of life—indisputable—inscribed in stone like Moses' commandments. But really it is just a code for coexistence. Morality is at the source of the concept of right and wrong and has become everyman's personal censor board. Life is neutral. It is what is—an organic unfolding. It is the idea of right and wrong that clefts us, the living, into two halves—the good and the bad—and leaves us with a heavy cross of guilt and shame to bear. Once I see that morality is just a code that has taken us over, I can be free of the shackles of guilt and shame. The spirit is beyond morality.

Spirituality is wholeness—an all-encompassing completeness. All I have to do to become whole and complete again is to retrieve my disavowed parts. How can I be whole without owning my whole self? I need to undertake a journey back from becoming to being. That journey is a journey inwards. The day I can look beyond morality and understand that good and bad are mental constructs; that God is all there is—God is everything—the good, the bad and the indifferent—I will be able to see divinity in my so-called darkness. I agree with R. Buckminster Fuller when he says, 'God, to me, it seems, is a verb not a noun.' God is not an entity but the very process of life and living. Jean-Claude Koven elaborates on the thought brilliantly, "God is indeed a verb. He is not the creator. He is the ongoing unfolding of creation itself.

There is nothing that is not a part of this unfolding. Thus there can be nothing separate from God . . . As you begin to view God not as the creator but as the constantly changing dance of creation itself, you'll discover him in everything you see—including yourself."

"Yatha pinde tatha brahmande"
"As is the microcosm so is the macrocosm"

—Upanishads

# Oneness

This story challenges us to think beyond the realm of time because according to this, creation is not a historical event; the universe is a spontaneous manifestation of desire.

**One is all there is, call it the field of potentiality. Just as a tiny seed carries within it the possibility of a massive tree complete with roots, trunk, branches and leaves—so also this One is the seed of creation, a potentiality for every conceivable thing. But unlike a seed, it is a formless energy field with no physicality. One was abiding in a state of powerful inertia called** *turiya* or pure bliss. Being formless, it enjoys the limitlessness of infinity and eternity because only the physical is subject to definitions of time and space and the laws of existence—birth, atrophy and death. Infinity and eternity are all very well, but this changeless, eventless continuum where nothing happens—pure bliss notwithstanding—gets a little boring, wouldn't you agree?

Enter desire—the desire for experience! Desire is the much-needed impulse for movement, for action, for the play of cause and effect and a cue for the game to begin. In order to experience, the One takes on a physical form, *and* splits into an explosion of multiplicity (shades of the Big Bang theory?) What defies human logic, located, or rather locked in the space-time dimension, is that this is not a historical event that happened once upon a time. The two states—*turiya* or pure bliss and the manifest physical universe—are spontaneous and simultaneous, coexisting like light and shade. This is the cosmic rhythm of creation and resolution—the play of light and shade; of appearance and reality; of oneness and plurality—the grand *Leela* or the game.

Being formless, the One is actually *no* thing—nothing. This is paradoxically the same as 'everything'—just as space, which is nothing; but contains the omniverse. Duality, or the world of opposites is an illusion that collapses at the meeting point of 'nothing' and 'everything'; of zero and infinity.

## Insight

1. Life is a single organism.
2. The One Life is its own purpose.
3. Each one of us *is* the One Life—self-caused; self-perpetuating; formless; infinite and eternal at source. To paraphrase Eckhart Tolle, we don't *have* a life, we *are* Life.
4. There is Life, with a capital 'L', comprised of zillions of units of life. The purpose of each individual life is to perpetuate the larger organism—Life.
5. Sometimes it may require the individual unit to survive while other times it may require the individual unit to perish in order to perpetuate the larger entity.

# The Design of Existence

*Man, of all species, is the most gregarious animal. No other system of cooperation and cohabitation is quite as intricate as human civilization. This being so, an understanding of our due place in the world is crucial. We live a dual existence consisting of two simultaneous lives—the organic life of physical survival and the notional life of psychological survival.*

There is life, as in existence, and there is life as only we humans know it. While the existential life is purely a phenomenon of nature, the alternate life of morality, culture, scientific inventions, political and economic structures—in a word, civilization, is a creation of the human mind. Of course the human mind is also a product of nature and therefore, in a larger sense, the alternate life too is a part of phenomenal existence but there seems to be a huge component of human will in the co-creation of this alternate life. Alongside existential life, the human mind has spawned a virtual existence so we humans have a physical existence *and* an additional psychological existence. This is a world of mental constructs made up of concepts and ideas. Survival in this virtual existence is not physical but conceptual survival. We have one physical identity but in the psychological realm we have multiple identities derived from our multifarious roles. We can die only one physical death but we can die a "thousand deaths"—as the phrase goes—psychologically.

"I'm finished" in this domain does not connote extinction but the breakdown of a theoretical construct, say, of my image as a successful business person, a super-star or a person revered for virtuous conduct. This parallel life is a shadow of the physical life and like the shadow, it has no physicality but its existence is undeniable. Pleasure and pain in this domain are not physical but emotional such as the pleasure of being appreciated and the pain of being rejected. This alternate life is largely defined by human mind along with all its attendant emotional responses. It is the stuff of human drama.

While all other life forms are body-spirit, we humans are a triad of body-mind-spirit. What sets us apart from the animal kingdom is a faculty of the mind called the intellect. Intellect is fine, except that it is inversely proportionate to another very useful faculty called instinct. As intellect develops, instinct diminishes. The more intellectual we get the less instinctual we are. That is why an animal instinctively knows a poison berry without ever having been told or read about it. We humans, on the other hand, have lost our instinctual intelligence and rely on information for our choice of berries. But the intellect has its uses in the alternate life—it is what gave us the grand artifice called civilization. One of its primary tools is memory—which comes in very useful for structural continuity and the discipline of organized activity. Despite scientific inventions being ascribed to certain individuals, no scientific invention would have been possible without recorded memory of the body of work before it. The credited inventors just happened to add the last few pieces, of the jigsaw to complete the picture.

The existential life is the organic life of very few needs—what Baloo the bear calls ". . . the simple 'bear' necessities of life" in the famous song from *Jungle Book*. It is the animal life of physical survival. It really *is* quite simple—it may have its share of struggle and hard work but it is not complicated. It has a one-point agenda—survival. The existential life demands nothing of us but to sustain and nurture life, both at the individual level and at the level of species. This agenda is driven through instinct and urges—hunger urge and self-preservation instinct for individual survival and sexual urge for the perpetuation of the species. So the only 'to do' in this domain is to satisfy the urges and follow the instincts because the survival instinct is too deeply ingrained to be compromised by intellect. Of course, there are instances of our emotional-intellectual faculty overriding even this instinct such as dying for honour—in war or peace; committing suicide for loss of face etc. but by and large, this instinct continues to work like a reflex for the preservation of life.

The existential life is purely the lifespan—the much spoken of dash between the date of birth and the date of death. In this domain, the mere existence of a creature has a bearing in the universal scheme of things and in the evolutionary flow of life. What happens between the two events is inconsequential and of no significance. Here, individual life is a unit of a larger entity which is the One Life with a capital L. Just as the body is made up of zillions of living units called cells, every creature that lives or ever lived, is a unit of the grand phenomenon of One Life. It would make no difference to my life if some cells of my body were to become famous amongst the cell world for discoveries and inventions or for writing epics—at the existential level they served their purpose just by coming into existence when they were required to and perishing when their term was over. A very important aspect of the One Life is that it is its own purpose—the purpose is to live. Without grasping this it is not possible to grasp its significance—its purpose is just to be. It counts not for the quality of its being but purely for being.

This thought is completely abhorrent to another faculty of intellect called discernment. Discernment is the faculty that makes qualitative judgments. It is concerned not with the lifespan but with the quality of that span. Here, the individual life counts not for just being but for doing, achieving, accomplishing, surmounting and for leaving behind a legacy. If survival instinct drives physical existence, identity-enhancement drives psychological existence. This faculty has created scales—of physical attributes—tall-short; thin-fat; dark-fair; good looking-ugly; well formed-deformed etc; and of mental fitness—normal-abnormal; sane-insane; dumb-intelligent-genius. These created scales and standards are not intrinsic to life for life makes no such distinctions—a monkey is a monkey—it doesn't matter how its facial features were put together; its physical size doesn't matter; its mental faculties are of no consequence. *It just is.* An animal does not have a sense of individual identity. It is a unit of the whole, called the universe. Just as a mass of water is made up of many, many integrated drops of water, an animal is an integral unit of nature. In nature, survival instinct serves the survival of the larger organism—the One Life. So the individual animal is perpetuating Life, whether it kills for hunger or becomes prey to another animal's hunger.

The faculty of discernment creates a sense of separation and individuality. The difference between humans and animals is that animals are integrated drops of the ocean of life without an individual identity while humans are the individual drops, separated and disconnected from the ocean. The separation happened when we extracted ourselves from the cycle of life—the food chain, and created an alternate existence. Reality is all-encompassing and all-inclusive; it is what is, exactly as it is. Intellect likes to break down what is, label and confine it within categories. It imposes formats on reality, It clefts it into two—the good and the bad; the desirable and the undesirable and then it wants to keep one half of it and throw the other out the window. It wants the rose without the thorns. It is this confrontation with reality that keeps humans marking time on a hamster's wheel—interminably going round and round. And so starts the saga of the doing-life which is a constant effort to change, improve, fix. Some Indian sages have referred to this alternate life as *Maya*—the grand illusion but I prefer to call it *Leela*—the game. Maya too, is a relevant term, as the alternate life is made up of nothing but abstract notions—morality, love, honour, fame, and success are mental constructs with no physical reality. But all these have come to acquire such a huge significance in the mental-emotional domain that to term it as illusion brings up a resistance. While the term *Leela*, or game, is not only a better analogy but also puts this alternate life in a balanced perspective. It is an appropriate analogy because like any other game, morality, love, honour, fame and success are based on agreed ground-rules and assumptions. The balanced perspective that the word *Leela* brings is that the alternate life is a game that we chose to play at some point in the history of our species. Once we are able to see that our social, civilized life is a game based on certain agreements and rules and not our helpless, ordained destiny we can stop taking it as seriously as we do.

At a generic level the function of all life forms is to survive and to evolve. Survival and evolution are inter-dependent—there is no evolution without survival and no survival without evolution. Evolution is an adaptation mechanism for survival in an ever-changing universe. Survival instinct is the basic program that drives us. Pain and pleasure are the mainstay of the survival instinct. The palate has been bestowed with the faculty of experiencing pleasure because eating is crucial to survival of the individual. The reproductive process is based on the pleasure principle because propagation is crucial to survival of the species. Likewise, pain is a survival mechanism—a warning signal to enable us to take care of some dysfunction in the body. But the game has taken us over. We have personalised pain and pleasure and woven it into a fabric of human drama. We are born into the game and painstakingly inducted into it early on, such that we don't notice existence. We humans have become all about doing and forgotten about the 'being' part of existence. 'Becoming' is always a movement away from who we are in our essence. New age spirituality attempts to re-connect us with this alienated centre—our real existential self through practices related to breath work, meditation and the like. Reflecting on this distinction of our two lives helps us to see each one for what it is and give each one its due place.

"You are here to enable the divine purpose of the universe to unfold. That is how important you are."

—Eckhart Tolle

# The Experience of Being Alive

A king once had a commoner friend who was very enamoured of royalty. The commoner friend always wanted to know what it felt like to have everything and to live in the lap of luxury. The king invited him to live in the palace for a few days and see for himself. So the friend arrived at the palace and was royally indulged with luxurious comforts, the finest cuisine and the best entertainment. "Wow," he said to the king, "Royalty is so much fun—I really envy you your life!"

"Wait a second!" the king exclaimed, "You have no idea about my life—if you really want to know how *I* enjoy royalty, I will show you tomorrow. Meet me in the palace foyer at eight o'clock in the morning if you want a taste of my life."

"Wow again!" thought the friend, "There's More!" and went to bed full of curiosity and anticipation. Next morning he was at the palace foyer way before the appointed time. The king entered the foyer at exact eight and said to his friend, "The pre-lunch program starts with a rendition of classical music by the famous maestro in my private auditorium at half past eight; after that there is display of the rarest and most beautiful flowers in the royal garden; that will be followed by a pageant of different bridal costumes donned by the ten most beautiful women of my kingdom. You don't have to worry about the timings and directions, my attendants will usher you from venue to venue well in time." Handing over a bowl of oil full to the brim, he continued, "Just take this along everywhere and make sure you don't spill a drop through all of this. We will meet at lunch and then I will tell you about my post-lunch schedule." The friend took the bowl and followed the king's attendants to the venue of the music concert.

When the two met at lunch, the king asked his friend how he enjoyed the morning. "All my attention was focused on not spilling the oil from the bowl that you gave me—there was none left to pay to any of those programs. How could I have enjoyed myself?" retorted the friend.

## Insight

1.  Beyond the obvious 'moral' of the story viz. "Only the wearer knows where the shoe pinches"; and "All that glitters is not gold" etc, I get that we can and must consciously choose what we put our attention to and how much.
2.  When we give all our attention to any one aspect of life like success, achievement, making a living, we miss out on the experience of being alive.
3.  We then live life in absentia and are missing from our own life.

# The Design of Humanity

*Not content with who we are we keep trying to compensate with what we have. In the process, human-being has become human-doing.*

Life means different things to different people; and different things to us at different times. It can mean ambition, fame, making a difference, achievement, success, doing good, growth, self-improvement, creativity, pursuit of excellence or happiness—any one or more of these. Most of these goals and aspirations are borrowed from the prevailing value systems. We buy into the value culture prevalent in our surroundings without examining their relevance in our personal value hierarchy. The operational word for the existential life is being and for the alternate mental-intellectual life it is doing. In Hindu philosophy the alternate life has been referred to as *'Karma Bhoomi'*—the domain of action. In this domain, one is defined by action such that even not doing connotes a kind of doing—*doing* nothing. There is no escaping karma here because failure to act is also karma and has its consequences. This is the domain of constant improvement with perfection as its holy grail. The alternate life of intellect dominates human attention and the perception that prevails is that the 'human doing' is the big brother, the guardian of 'human being'—that we owe our being to our doing. But does that thought hold true? Just as breathing happens

without any conscious effort on our part, life happens—
we don't do life. The wheels of evolution are grinding to
perpetuate Life. Within this process of evolution, the human
species developed a complex brain mechanism called the
mind. The hallmark of mind is control—so it began by
wresting the responsibility for survival from nature. We
extracted ourselves from the food-chain eliminating our
vulnerability to predators. We don't depend on nature's
bounty but 'cultivate' food for our consumption be it grains
from fields or livestock from animal farms. We created
community living and a culture of cooperation for security
and safety of life and put a medical system in place for
preservation of life. All this creates a sense of control. We
feel in control because we seem to have assumed full charge
of ourselves—we don't seem to depend on nature for our
survival—we produce our own food, protect ourselves
from the vagaries of nature. But here's a thought—isn't the
development of human mind also within the evolutionary
flow? We often pitch ourselves as equal to nature, even if
negatively, when we speak of man v/s nature. To me that is
a very presumptuous thought. How can man—a creation
of nature—be pitched as its equal? How can there be 'man
v/s nature' when man is a product of nature? Humans have
assumed ownership of intellect and the impression seems to
be that we *used* our intellect to create this whole domain of
alternate life without nature having any role in it. But how
can we take credit for our intellect—which, like the wings
of birds, is a gift of evolution. It is more like we have *been
used* by the process of evolution, to create this paradigm of
civilization through the instrument of intellect. Nothing
happens or can happen outside of nature and without its
consent—civilization, along with the paraphernalia of the

alternate existence, is a stage in the evolutionary scheme of things.

The evolutionary impulse is not focused on any individual unit of life or on any one species. Human-doings tend to see themselves as chosen—on both the individual level and at the level of species. This is the genesis of the notion of man being at the centre of the universe—the chosen one. It also extends to a sense of importance of our species—we perceive ourselves as special and on top of the evolutionary ladder.

"Let us make man in our image, after our likeness; and let them have dominion over the fish of the sea, and over the birds of the air, and over the cattle, and over all the earth, and over every creeping thing that creeps upon the earth. So God created man in his own image, in the image of God he created him; male and female he created them. And God blessed them, and God said to them, "Be fruitful and multiply, and fill the earth and subdue it; and have dominion over the fish of the sea and over the birds of the air and over every living thing that moves upon the earth."—Genesis 1:26.

Did God create man in his own image or did man create God in his image has been a subject of debate but this notion of our position in the scheme of things and of oneself at the centre of the universe challenges us repeatedly.

Making a distinction between the two lives—existential or physical and mental or psychological helps us put both in perspective. The psychological life has taken up too much of our attention and we have become mental creatures (pun intended) living completely in our heads. We "live up there and slightly to one side" as Sir Ken Robinson humorously puts it; so much so that we "look upon [our] body as a means of transport for [our] heads." We need to contemplate on this askew emphasis on what is just one aspect of life which is multi-faceted.

"I can find only three kinds of business in the universe: mine, yours and God's . . . When you think that someone or something other than yourself needs to change, you're mentally out of your business."

—Byron Katie

# Reality Check

This is the oft-repeated story of four blind men who once wanted to know what an elephant is like.

Four blind men were the greatest of friends. All of them were very keen on knowledge and learning. They read Braille books together and loved to discuss what they learnt. One day, they read about an elephant and decided to find out what an elephant was like. So off they went to the circus and got themselves a special permission to get up-close to touch and feel the animal and to know firsthand what an elephant is like. The attendant guided them to the enclosure of the elephant and they started to advance towards it all in a row, arms outstretched.

The first blind man got to the trunk. He felt it up and down and muttered to himself, "Funny, an elephant is a lot like a snake!"

"An elephant is like a tree trunk!" thought the second blind man with his arms round the animal's leg.

The third blind man, who was the tallest amongst them all, felt the expanse of the elephant's torso and murmured, "An elephant is huge and flat—like a whale!"

While the fourth blind man held the elephant's tail and said to himself, "Strange! It seems the elephant is like a rope."

## Insight

1. We all have our own separate story which arises out of how we experience life.
2. We live cocooned inside a story called, "I know".
3. What I know is, no doubt, the truth but not the whole truth and certainly not the universal truth. What I know is just my own subjective truth.
4. But I don't think so.
5. I think that what I know is Truth with a capital T, which is everybody else's truth too and that is why I am confused, angry and incredulous when people don't agree with me.
6. 'Snake', 'tree trunk', 'whale' and 'rope' are all valid in part but none of these capture the truth of what an elephant is.
7. A viewpoint is never right or wrong. However bizarre it may sound, it is valid—as a viewpoint.
8. What is wrong is our mistaken belief that our viewpoint is reality.
9. And therefore it is, or should be everyone else's reality too.
10. This mistaken belief is the illusion that makes life so baffling.
11. Let us hold what we know lightly and tentatively and at least consider where 'what others know' comes from.
12. Our partial truth (which we think is the whole truth) is constantly at odds with others' partial truth (which they think is the whole truth).

13. Obviously there is no agreement—one says 'snake' another says 'tree trunk' and the third says 'whale' when, in fact, they are all talking about an elephant.
14. Welcome to the circus . . .

# The Design of Reality

*Objective reality is unknowable. All we can ever have access to is realityscape—our subjective view of reality.*

We humans access reality through our five senses and a brain that processes the sensory information and collates it with memory of past experience. On the one hand our understanding of reality is far greater than any one of the four blind men who described the reality of an elephant through their limited experience of it. On the other, if, hypothetically speaking, there are several more senses than five, or even one more sense that we lack, then our perception of reality is definitely handicapped. A blind person cannot even begin to comprehend what vision is because a sensory experience can never be communicated through language. Concepts like light and darkness; colours and shades—a whole world of visual experience and what it can add to one's comprehension of the world is unavailable to him. Likewise, we may be severely challenged in our comprehension of the world without those hypothetical extra senses.

Apart from being limited to five, each one of our senses is limited to a narrow bandwidth. We cannot see below and above a certain frequency of light. Our hearing is limited to a certain range of decibels. Our tactile sense often doesn't register a mosquito bite till an itch or a rash appears. Given the limitation of our sense receptors it is obvious that our access to reality is limited. That being so, we can hypothesise about the true nature of reality but we can never really be sure about reality as an absolute, objective, factual state of things. Robert Frost's famous couplet is the best enunciation of this thought:

"We dance round in a ring, and suppose.

But the secret sits in the middle, and knows."

Reality is the unknowable secret. The point is that un-interpreted reality exists as a mere concept. It cannot be owned or possessed. The famous philosophical riddle, "If a tree falls in a forest and no one is around to hear it, does it make a sound?" points to the myth of absolute reality. Unmitigated reality is a mere notion—a theoretical construct. The moment it is expressed by anyone, it becomes that person's reality—his point of view. Absolute, objective reality is unknowable because objectivity is a mere notion—we can only extrapolate, guess and infer objective reality but the moment anyone takes ownership of it, it becomes his or her reality. An understanding of this distinction is crucial to an understanding of relationship at any level. It is the basis of all conflict, be it interpersonal, inter-social, inter-cultural, inter-religious or inter-national. The argument of the four blind men is the quintessential analogy for all differences.

Realityscape is different from reality—it is the view of reality from our window to the world. It is reality as it occurs to us. In other words, it is the windowscape of the skyline of reality, available to us. By its very definition realityscape is a limited view. Realityscape—our personal view of reality—

poses a problem on two counts to create conflict. First is the assumption that my realityscape *is* reality. Second, for that very reason, my realityscape is shared by everyone.

So realityscape is our personal interpretation of reality. It is an ever-evolving world view—dynamic and constantly changing like the kaleidoscope. It is shaped and reshaped by our internal response to external stimulus moment to moment. Constantly in a flux, it is an ongoing interaction between existing content of the mind and new information. Realityscape is an intensely personal world view that we live inside of, believe in and operate from. In simple phraseology it is closest in description to 'belief system' and 'operating paradigm'. My realityscape is not just what is before me in the now moment. It is a construct of what I sense in the now moment, *filtered* through my earlier experience and coloured by my emotional overtones. So realityscape is complex, personal and purely experiential. As unique as our fingerprint, it is a world view that we think we share with every other human being; but like the fingerprint, it is singularly unique in specifics.

Despite the very profound statement of Einstein that "E is equal to mc square" *and* the ripple effect of 'the theory of relativity' on philosophy, we humans have a minimal understanding of subjectivism. This is not a judgment, just an evaluation of our current situation in the evolution of consciousness—we, at both the individual and the collective level, are infantile when it comes to understanding subjectivity. We just cannot comprehend the maxim that life is just a perspective—nothing more; nothing less. Embedded deep in our psyche is a complex belief system that we didn't even choose in the first place. This belief system is unique to every individual, much like the fingerprints. What makes this belief system so uniquely personal is the interplay of personal preferences with the multiple layers of familial, societal, cultural, religious, political, spiritual and other conditionings that we are subjected to from day one. Our commitment to this belief system that we didn't even choose in the first place, is so deep that it is the only thing many of us would, and have laid down, *and* taken lives for. Not only are we helplessly and hopelessly tied to this complex of belief systems but we also take them to be universally true. This inevitably leads to the need to 'correct' those who don't subscribe to our way of thinking while those others are already looking to 'correct' us.

Welcome to the circus!

The assumption behind the need to 'correct' or 'convert' another to our way of thinking is that there is a 'right way' out there that everyone ought to adhere to, and that happens to be my way. While a singular belief system or universal terms of agreement would definitely make things a lot easier and smoother, it would also, perhaps make life very dull and boring. It would be the end of debate and discussion—what would we possibly talk about if all agreed? It would be the end of variety—which is undoubtedly the spice of life, and life would be one monotonous mono tone—which was the reason we manifested multiplicity from the pre-creation Oneness in the first place. The Chinese symbol for yin and yang would then be a boring all-black or all-white circle. So while consensus is definitely not the answer, conflict needs to be dealt with an understanding of subjectivity. All we need to agree on is disagreement. We need to learn to contain diversity—of faith, belief and culture, and of ideologies and philosophies. We need to experiment with allowing opposing and paradoxical viewpoints to coexist—the trick being not to impose or convert; to realize that differences are not contradictions; that we don't have to duel it out because you say X and I say Y, and that X and Y, like ebony and ivory, can live in perfect harmony. Also, we need to teach and learn freedom of choice and choose our beliefs freely instead of being so hopelessly tied to the un-chosen ones.

"The belief that there is only one truth and that oneself is in possession of it seems to me the deepest root of all evil that is in the world."

—MAX BORN

# Choice is Freedom

Buddha was once walking the village street with his disciples when suddenly a man appeared from nowhere and started yelling at him. He hurled all manner of abuses, insults and allegations against the master and just wouldn't stop. The Buddha was completely unfazed and just stood there waiting for the man to finish, but the irate man carried relentlessly on. A crowd gathered around while the one-sided tirade continued. Finally, when the man had exhausted his reserve of anger and run out of expletives, he turned to leave.

The disciples stood rooted waiting for a response of some kind—perhaps a transformative discourse. But to their surprise, even the Buddha turned to leave.

"What was that—why did you take all that?" the disciples wanted to know.

"Well, that's precisely what I didn't do," replied the master, "I exercised choice and decided not to take what that angry young man brought me; and yet," the Buddha continued, "by listening without resistance or opposition, I emptied him of his anger."

# Insight

1. We don't have to catch every ball that's thrown at us.
2. We can pause to choose our response in any situation instead of giving a knee-jerk reaction.
3. We are hurt by other people's negative perception of us only because we want to control what people think of us.
4. We don't have an independent sense of self—we derive our sense of self from what others think of us.
5. That is why we are easily swayed and disturbed by 'opinions'.
6. Our upsets have everything to do with that and very little to do with others and their opinion of us.
7. Freedom is nothing but the right to choose—if I am confined forcefully, I am not free because I have been deprived of the choice to move around so, by that logic, choice is freedom. But the reverse is also true—freedom is choice. If I surrender to my confinement and thereby accept it or in other words 'choose' it—then I am free even in confinement.
8. Last, but not the least, I can see the validity of 'bending with the blow'—a martial arts strategy—in every confrontation. I can exercise choice and let the blow pass over my head by not taking up a position in a confrontation—for what you resist will definitely persist.

# The Design of Belief

*Fixed interpretations of a dynamic reality give us our out-dated beliefs and operating paradigms.*

Beliefs are the raw stock of human drama. A belief is the only thing a human will ever lay down or take life for—be it a terrorist on a death mission or a person who commits suicide out of a sense of shame or dishonour—the cause is inextricably linked to a belief. Without our knowing it, a belief is our most prized possession.

Belief is both the genesis as well as the nemesis of humanity: genesis because it is our distinguishing feature—it is a belief-system that sets humans apart from other species and one human being from another; nemesis because a belief on being possessed, takes over and becomes the possessing entity. Each one of us carries a unique complex of beliefs and every time there is disagreement with another's beliefs, we feel threatened and invalidated. Sartre summed up this predicament of humanity in his famous line—'Hell is other people'. Beliefs make us lose the freedom of choice; we become positional, stuck, fossilized in time. This is true not only of our bigger belief systems like religious, political, ideological or philosophical but of every single thought and opinion. Virtue and morality, for instance, are mere conventions—a code of conduct devised for co-habitation of the human race. Every notion of right and wrong stems from that code which is nothing but an agreement—like the rules of a game. But our belief that virtue, right and wrong are intrinsic, is so deep-seated that we just cannot bring ourselves to think of them as mere agreements. So what we think of as a belief may merely be an agreement.

Our complete belief in the absoluteness and universality of what we believe is at the root of all conflict. In fact, the unquestioned belief that what we believe is the absolute, universal truth is the real problem. It has never occurred to us to question the validity of our beliefs because they appear on our mental horizon as Truths with a capital T. We equate our thoughts or beliefs with knowing. Long years ago, before Copernicus, we believed that the sun revolves around the earth. So steeped were we in that belief that Copernicus nearly got laughed out of the renaissance when he suggested otherwise. Now we believe that it is the earth that revolves around the sun—who knows if that belief will also be challenged some day! If there are rumbles of disagreement about how there is irrefutable, conclusive proof that the earth does indeed revolve around the sun—it only goes to prove my point that we are inextricably entwined with what we believe.

Einstein's theory of relativity put paid to the very idea of objective reality. Then Quantum physics put a question mark on the materiality of matter. The Hindu concept of Maya or illusion—nothing is what it appears to be—has been vindicated and endorsed by science. In fact, one of the early stages of the awakening process is the recognition of the delusion that I am at the centre of the universe in sole possession of 'the truth'. It is the realization that truth is inclusive, not exclusive; that there is my truth and there is your truth and that all truths are valid points-of-view. The matrix of life is a series of contracts and agreements that we are born into. Life, as we know it, is based on certain assumptions which over time have become unquestionable truisms. We are born into a world of pre-fabricated structures—structures of knowledge; structures of values; structures of morality; legal, political, economic and religious structures. We inherit a world of agreements and contracts that are binding on us even though we did not enter into these personally. The structures of religion and culture, for instance, get chosen for us by virtue of our parentage while the legal, political and economic structures come with our geographic location—the state or the country we live in. These various structures are made up of dos and don'ts that, over time, come to be regarded as intrinsic to life, but they are not. Seeing how this eclectic mix of customs, conventions, laws etc. that regulate and rule our life came to be, puts life in perspective and helps us see them for what they really are. It may not change the way we live but it will definitely change the way we see life.

Law and code of morality are agreements specific to different countries and different cultures. There is no right or wrong independent of the context of agreements—our shared belief system. Apart from our shared belief systems we have our individual value system which is the hierarchy of value we put on different 'virtues'. Conflict is a clash of either shared belief systems or individual value systems. This is the basis for every argument, disagreement and conflict ever. Personal belief is a synthesis of cultural, social and political agreements that we were born into on the one hand, and our physical and emotional blueprint or DNA on the other.

Because we are born to these agreements, in other words because the matrix of agreements exist before the event of our birth, they are so compelling and seem so intrinsic to life. Our upbringing, conditioning and programming is completely focused on teaching and training us to comply. In order to sanctify this compliance, the concept of virtue and of right and wrong is brought in. The fear of God—reward and punishment (incentives and deterrents) are created at different levels. At first level compliance gets you nods of approval—so appearing good becomes not just an incentive but an addiction. Actually enough of an addiction as is evident from the fact that only a minority of us needs to be dealt with at the next level of enforcement. At first level it is fear of disapproval and reward of acclaim. Next level is the legal enforcement. If somebody is not deterred by fear of punishment then in certain contexts law intervenes to keep agreements in place. Alongside, it is fear of God or religion that keeps agreements in place.

We tend to confuse 'believing' with 'knowing'—so what is a belief and what is knowledge? The dictionary meaning of belief is "a statement, principle, or doctrine that a person or group accepts as true" while knowledge is "clear awareness or explicit information, e.g. of a situation or fact". Going by these meanings, a belief is subjective and personal, but knowledge is objective and factual—it has a closer relationship with reality. In our past paradigm about the shape of the earth—is its flatness or roundness a matter of belief or knowledge? Like everything else in the universe, knowledge too is subject to the law of evolution. In the past our knowledge, based on a body of assumptions, said the earth is flat. Fresh evidence and deductions unfolded and replaced that version of the earth's shape with round. So knowledge too is dynamic, ever in flux, it grows, changes, unfolds and gets revealed over time. We can never hit the bull's eye with this moving target. All we can ever have access to, is our current view of reality at any given time. Today when we know the earth to be round, we operate from that premise just as we operated from the premise of 'flat' back then and wouldn't charter fresh waters for fear of falling off the edge of the earth. The point is that knowledge is tentative—something to hold on to till it is either disproven or replaced by new discoveries, insights, understanding, paradigm shift etc.

The problem arises when we hold knowledge tightly in our fists and convert it into a belief. A belief is knowledge fossilised—we strangulate knowledge when we strait jacket it into our belief system; it stops breathing and growing. Knowledge needs to be used like the air we breathe. We take it in, use it and breathe it out. We don't hold it in our lungs forever for fear of annihilation. We breathe it out making room for another breath of fresh air. Similarly, beliefs should be breathed; held lightly, tentatively and be exchanged for fresh ones, so we can grow.

"Life is like a game of cards. The hand you are dealt is determinism; the way you play it is free will."

—Jawaharlal Nehru

# Life knows best

Once a king and his Prime Minister were the best of friends. Being childhood buddies, they spent pretty much all their time together. During the day they were together attending to the business of the kingdom and by night they would get entertained together—hunting, playing chess or watching cultural performances.

The minister had a favourite catchphrase that he was in the habit of uttering, whatever the occasion. Come hail or sunshine, disaster or good tidings, he would utter the same line whatever happened. The phrase was "All for the best!"

The king and his courtiers were only too familiar with this habit and nobody ever took the catchphrase literally. One day, however, the king was inspecting an arrow-head and accidentally severed his little finger. Much royal blood was lost and the king was in great pain when his friend, the minister came on the scene. Upon learning about the accident, as he was wont to do, he uttered, "All for the best!" This once, the king, irritable as he already was, flew into a rage. "What do you mean 'All for the best'—how insensitive and uncaring of you! You deserve to be neither my friend nor minister! Get out of my sight!"

The minister stood in complete silence looking quite remorseless, which didn't help matters. The king's ire notched up another scale, "Throw him into the jail!" he thundered.

"All for the best!" mumbled the minister from sheer force of habit as he was taken into custody by the royal guards.

The king was slated to go on a hunt that evening with his friend, the minister. Despite the way the day had turned out, he thought he would go ahead with the plan anyway, just to cheer himself up. So he set off on horseback with his retinue. Disturbed and distracted as the king was, he somehow broke away from his group and suddenly found himself alone in a clearing in the forest. Dusk was already upon him when he realized he was lost and so he decided to find a riverside to camp by for the night—hoping that his hunting team would find him soon enough. As he cantered along in search of water, he saw a light in the distance. Relieved, he galloped towards the light which turned out to be a big bonfire around which a tribal group was dancing. Upon seeing the king, they immediately seized him. They tied his hands behind his back and pushed him into the centre and resumed dancing around him. To his horror, the king soon realized that they meant to offer him up in sacrifice to the fire god.

Presently, they untied his hands to offer him up as sacrifice, when one of them noticed his severed finger. They started clucking and saying that they could not offer him since the sacrifice would be incomplete because of his missing finger. So they let him go and continued to appease the fire god with their dance. The king ran to his horse, mounted it in one swift movement and bolted for his life. Soon enough he was found by his hunting party and together they headed back for the palace.

This incident shook up the king real bad. He kept thinking back on how he almost lost his life. Then suddenly, he made the connection between what had happened and what his friend, the minister, had said. He ordered for his friend to be released and presented before him.

"You were right, my friend," said the king, "When you said what you always say. It was indeed 'for the best' that my finger got cut off considering it saved my life. But tell me, you said the same thing again when you were being taken away to be thrown into the jail, you spent a miserable night in the jail—how was that 'for the best'?"

"If you really think about it that too was 'for the best'! Had I not been in jail, I would have been with you last evening. Since we always ride side by side, we would have got lost together. The tribal folk would have spared you because of your severed finger and they would have offered me up as sacrifice instead."

## Insight

1. Life has a logic of its own which sometimes we can understand only in hindsight and sometimes not at all.
2. Trusting whatever unfolds is the only sensible way to be.

# The Design of Free Will

*Do we live life or is life lived through us? Is doer-ship an illusion?*

At the other end of the spectrum of free-will are two concepts—destiny and determinism. Certain streams of spiritual philosophy consider destiny or karma the opposite of free will. This is the play of cause and effect which unfolds as life. According to this, every action or non-action has a consequence and every moment that unfolds, is an accrual of historical, personal, familial, and genetic karma. According to this, free will is a separatist need for control and it is a sure recipe for suffering. If individual will is completely aligned with the reality of the moment and surrenders to the organic unfolding of the universal design then there is no conflict, no disappointment, no frustration and consequently, no suffering. But psychology has a different version of what is in the way of free will—determinism. According to this, the personality we get shaped into is our programming and determines our action leaving little room for free will. Our compulsive attributes like rage, lust, greed, inhibition etc. sometimes overtake prudence and make us act in irrational and self-destructive ways. These deterministic attributes rob us of free will and change the course of our chosen trajectory. So while giving up the sense of control and doer-ship is the philosophical solution, working on personality and gaining control over our compulsive patterns is what psychology recommends.

Despite the faculty of intellect, which helps us make informed choices, there is a huge factor of programming arising out of our conditioning that gives us a fixed, often un-chosen way of being. Our personality limits our choices and therefore our freedom. We give knee-jerk reactions more out of the helpless need of our personality mould than out of the need of the hour. A meek person is completely perplexed by his aggressive friend's response to a situation when he says, "If I were you I would have punched his nose." The meek one may "inherit the earth" but punching someone's nose is not even an option for him. The point is that each one of us is restricted by his or her personality and cannot behave outside the allowances of one's personality. The famous theme of antithetical twins in movies illustrates this idea of personality traps very effectively. While the meek twin cannot bring him or herself to be assertive despite being advantageously placed; the assertive twin cannot even pretend to be meek. The question then is: what is the extent of free will in human life and can it be enhanced?

Reinhold Niebuhr's much-quoted Serenity Prayer acknowledges the boundaries of determinism and free will:

God, grant me the serenity to accept the things I cannot change,

Courage to change the things I can,

And wisdom to know the difference.

Clearly, there are things we can do something about and things we can't do anything about but the last line points to the dilemma of not always knowing the demarcation.

So how do we humans 'go beyond' the limitation of our programming? According to psychology it all starts with an acknowledgement and awareness of our programming in the first place. This acknowledgement is the gateway—the portal that gives us the access to go beyond. When we act from "I couldn't help it", be it flying into a rage or becoming distraught or whatever, we are acting from our program. All we need to do is to notice these unconscious actions and reactions and observe the personality traps that all of us live inside of. When we become aware of the concept of the deterministic role of personality, initially it is easier to look at personality traps of others, but if we stay with the observation, we begin to see our own as well. This practice of observing ourselves, automatically gives us an access to transcend our programming and the limitations of our personality. Slowly we become aware of the programmed parts of our personality. Once the programming comes under observation, a gap is created between the person that I am and the program that runs me. This is the beginning of free-will. When we throw the light of consciousness on the unexamined, compulsive patterns that drive us and start working on them, we slowly come unshackled. But this is never a water-shed event—it's a sustained process. One must keep chipping away at the hardened shell of identity that covers our natural self, to experience liberation.

Spiritual thought does not recommend strengthening of free-will but surrendering to what unfolds as the universal design and giving it up altogether. According to this, the universe follows a divine agenda—which is beyond our comprehension. It cannot follow seven billion individual agendas. So an individual always loses when his agenda clashes with the universal unfolding and he suffers as consequence. To be "in the flow" is to surrender free-will to the divine will. When we do this, we are in a space of *turiy*a or pure bliss because total surrender leaves no room for frustration, disappointment, and suffering—this is what spiritual seekers aspire for.

"If you would be a real seeker after truth, it is necessary that at least once in your life you doubt, as far as possible, all things."

—Rene Descartes

# Enough

Long, long ago a king named Mayadas ruled over a prosperous kingdom in the North-Eastern part of India. He was a good king—meticulous to a fault. He always wanted to be in the know, in order to be on top of things. One day, a thought struck him, "I wonder what my material worth is." He tried to make some quick calculations but given the extent of his kingdom it wasn't easy. So he decided to go about it in a proper manner. He called his Prime Minister and ordered him to put the administrative machinery to work to calculate his net worth.

"Prepare a detailed list of every item in the royal treasury—gold, silver, coins and currency; evaluate the mines; calculate the value of land, the royal granary and whatever else has any value, and in one month, present before me an assessment of my total wealth."

The administration was thrown into a flurry. Frenzied calculations began. Every item in the treasury was listed and evaluated. Officials measured the royal fields. Estimates of un-mined minerals were prepared. Every sack of grain was weighed, counted and listed. After a month of frantic calculations, the Prime Minister was ready. On the appointed day, he presented before King Mayadas the consolidated figure of his total worth. The figure ran into so many digits that King Mayadas had no idea what sense to make of it and whether it was good or bad.

"Prepare another list based on my current expenditure as well as future projections and this time, tell me how long my wealth will last," He ordered.

Within a week, the estimates were prepared and once again the Prime Minister appeared before the king with his conclusion. "Your Majesty! As it stands today, your wealth is good enough to last for ten generations."

King Mayadas fainted.

The court was thrown into chaos. Someone got water and splashed it on the king's face and he half opened his eyes. "What will become of my eleventh generation . . ." he mumbled and fainted again.

King Mayadas was carried to his sleeping chambers and left to recover under the supervision of the Raj-Vaid—the royal medicine man. The following days saw the king in a dejected and despondent state of mind. He wouldn't eat well, sleep well and began to lose health. The Raj-Vaid tried various formulations, but the king's health continued to fall.

Finally, the king's Guru was summoned. "Why so pale, king—what ails thee?," he asked.

"Guruji" replied the king, "I can't eat, sleep or relax because I'm worried that my eleventh generation will starve to death. You see, I only have enough wealth to last for ten generations. What should I do?"

"Only one person can answer your question—an old lady named Santushti/Serenity who lives at the edge of the forest, next to the Bodhi tree by the river. Go and pose the question to her and remember to take a sack of wheat for her," said the Raj-Guru.

The following morning, the king set out with a sack of wheat. Dusk had begun to set in by the time he reached Santushti/Serenity's hut. He knocked and the old woman opened the door.

"I am King Mayadas!" said the king by way of introduction. "My Raj-Guru has sent me to meet you."

"Of course!" said the old woman, "I extend a very warm welcome to you, king—please come in."

"Thank you! The Raj-Guru has sent you a sack of wheat," said the king signalling his men to bring it in.

"That's very kind of him—but before you have it brought in, let me check my larder," said the old woman.

Then she called out to her daughter in the kitchen, "Dear, how much wheat do we have left?"

"Enough for tonight, mother!" came the daughter's reply.

"Oh, please thank the Raj-Guru and tell him that I didn't need the wheat tonight," said Santushti/Serenity.

# Insight

1. Abundance is not the state of your larder; it's a state of mind.
2. 'Enough' does not pertain to quantity but to contentment.
3. Security is born of trusting life and living in the moment.
4. Life is a string of now moments—all we ever need to do is take care of this one moment.
5. There's no need to get ahead of ourselves and take care of a moment that's not here yet.

# The Design of Creativity

*Questioning is the portal to creative potential. Creativity stems from questioning.*

Have you ever noticed how a question exudes a dynamic energy—most unlike an answer? An answer lets you be. It doesn't ask anything of you. It doesn't seem to care whether you agree or disagree. A question, on the other hand, provokes you. It takes you along. It opens up possibilities—it invites interaction, it initiates a debate, it forges a relationship and abides with you. A question is dynamic; an answer is static. An interrogative mark at the end of a sentence has a 'to be continued' or a 'watch this space' feel as opposed to a period which is like a cul-de-sac. Questions are alive and full of creative potential. They are portals to discoveries and inventions, to growth and development. Every discovery and invention owes its origin to questioning—somebody somewhere questioned a given, and a new paradigm was born. We must question our automatic beliefs and paradigms— whether inherited, culturally imbibed or garnered from personal experience. Questioning opens up possibilities for out-of-the-box thinking. And yet, there is a premium laid on answers rather than on questions. Education system follows an information download model. There is no attempt to encourage or satisfy young curiosity. Again, law is a lot of answers that no one thinks to question. Eldon Taylor in

*What does That Mean,* which is an exhortation to think through questioning, explores the idea of capital punishment in the light of a series of relevant questions, "What if you learnt that capital punishment didn't deter crime? What if you knew that it cost much more to execute criminals than to warehouse them in solitary confinement? What if you learnt that lifelong isolation was more of a deterrent than being put to death?"

Questions precede answers, even pre-empt them, for every question is said to contain the answer. There can be questions without answers but there cannot be answers without questions. While an answer is like a closed door, a question opens up new avenues. We think of question-answer as a complete circuit, whereas an answer is merely a resting place. With a questioning attitude there is no arriving—not even at the Truth with a capital T. For incessant questioning takes you beyond—to newer truths. Rather than a QA circuit, life is a continuum of QAQAQAQ. Every discovery and invention owes its origin to that continuum. Answers provide stability and questions provide the momentum for growth and change. We tend to hold on to answers out of a need for security—the security of familiarity, of knowing and of certainty. Questions can be uncomfortable—because they leave us with a feeling of unfinished business. A question is perceived as a means to an end—the end being the answer whereas the answer too is a tentative place, not the destination. Answers are the ever changing patterns of a universe on the go—constantly moving on the wheels of evolution. They are like so many trapezes in the universal circus, to be given up for the next one before long. If you don't let go, you will have lost the chance to get to the next one. But giving up a trapeze involves that agonizingly fearful split second of being in the air without anything to hold on to. And that precisely is the discomfort we avoid by living in a world of answers, holding on to our beliefs for dear life.

We have too many answers and answers become beliefs if we hold on to them long enough. Then they begin to look deceptively like universal truths. The value of beliefs should be tentative—as in algebra where we assume values in order to make calculations. All self-growth work is ultimately about questioning our habitual way of looking at the world, breaking out of the default mode and for the first time choosing our perspective and stance.

"I believe that the brain has evolved over millions of years to be responsive to different kinds of content in the world. Language content, musical content, spatial content, numerical content etc."

—Howard Gardner

# What You Resist, Persists

There once lived a cunning medicine-man who claimed he could cure any illness under the sun. When someone came to him with an illness he could treat, he would give them a potion and cure them. When, however someone came with an illness he could not cure, he would employ a clever ruse to save his face. This ruse was based on a very astute understanding of the machinations of the human mind. He would prepare a potion and give it to the patient with the following instruction: "Remember," he would say, "this potion will work only on one condition. You are not to entertain any thought of monkey while taking this medicine."

What a self-defeating prescription! Now the dosage was inextricably linked to a taboo thought that would counter its benefit. Every time the patient would take the medicine, he would become conscious of the injunction and start chasing away mental monkeys.

## Insight

1. Injunction is not the best way to ensure compliance.
2. You can never fight a thought or wish it away.
3. The more you resist it, the more it persists.
4. Monkey thoughts are the thoughts that keep us grounded and are inextricably linked to our desire to fly.

# The Design of Learning

*IQ is a fraction of the intelligence spectrum. Mother Teresa's IQ, for instance, would have no bearing on her work whatsoever.*

Learning is the key to growth and development. Education is the building block of civilization. It is through sharing of thoughts and ideas that each generation stands on the shoulders of the previous one. The purpose of learning is to discover one's purpose in life. This is done by developing our uniqueness and reaching our full potential; by being the best we can be; by opening up and channelling our thinking faculties in creative ways.

Krishnamurti sums up the function of education beautifully in the following lines.

"Surely, education has no meaning unless it helps you to understand the vast expanse of life with all its subtleties, with its extraordinary beauty, its sorrows and joys. You may earn degrees; you may have a series of letters after your name and land a very good job, but then what? What is the point of it all if in the process your mind becomes dull, weary, stupid? So, while you are young, must you not seek to find out what life is all about. And is it not the true function of education to cultivate in you the intelligence which will try to find the answer to all these problems. Do you know what intelligence is? It is the capacity, surely, to think freely, without fear, without a formula, so that you begin to discover for yourself what is real, what is true."

Unfortunately, education today has been reduced to a numbers game. With admission cut-offs going not just through the roof but the sky, our education system has bred a culture of one-upmanship and cut-throat competition. Frenetic lifetimes are spent keeping up with the Joneses in complete disregard of our deep urges for expression which manifest as our talents. The grading and evaluation system of education is in a certain sense, the root cause of a world obsessed with success and competition. In an environment of competition there are ninety nine losers for one winner. The question to ask at this point in time when humanity is constantly striving for more and better, and not getting anywhere is, is comparison a relevant paradigm of evaluation? Shouldn't the education system evaluate individuals on the basis of individual learning curve rather than in comparison to others? Competitiveness sows the seeds of comparison and inadequacy early in life creating a needless polarity of success and failure. We spend our entire lives running a race without a finishing line in sight, constantly trying to 'match up' to, we are not sure what. In the process our natural talents are muffled early in life. The result is that true satisfaction forever eludes us. We then experience our inner void as a bottomless pit which we keep filling with accomplishments, achievements and acquisitions, but never arriving.

Apart from the flaws of comparative evaluation, the mass consumption design of modern education has taken the joy out of learning. The system is designed to push pre-set curriculums down students' throats. Like it or lump it! Pink Floyd's famous video, '*We don't need no education*' is a graphic depiction of how the current system of learning is making zombies out of us. Tagore called our schools factories—"At half past ten, in the morning the factory opens with the ringing of a bell, and then as the teachers start talking, the machines start working. The teachers stop talking at four in the afternoon when the factory closes and the pupils then go home carrying with them a few pages of machine made learning." He tried to revive the Indian educational tradition which goes back to the gurukuls—small learning groups which were highly personalised and informal. The gurukuls delivered holistic education, which was a harmonious package of knowledge, values, and skills.

In 1983 Dr. Howard Gardner wrote his ground-breaking book 'Multiple Intelligences' and forever changed our perception of intelligence. For the first time it showed us a much broader spectrum of intelligence of which IQ is just a fraction. IQ has been reigning supreme and has held a monopolistic sway over modern education system. Dr. Gardner's theory has shown us that an IQ-based education is one-dimensional and askew in that it treats a part as a whole. It completely disregards a whole world of talent outside the ambit of IQ, a whole world of talent that never reaches its potential because there is no recognition of it. Every child is born with a special gift but our IQ-centric perception doesn't allow us to recognise it. One child can be as different from another as an apple from an orange and so cannot be measured by the same yardstick. The current system of education not only fails to recognise each child's unique gift but also does a lot of damage by judging and labelling the non-IQ type as a failure. Dr. Gardner's theory suggests that, rather than relying on a uniform curriculum where 'one size fits all', a new system needs to be devised which should offer individual-centred education, with curriculum tailored to the needs of each child.

Based on the principle of mass production, the current system delivers as per the law of averages. A large group of students is expected to move at the same pace during an academic year in a variety of subjects. His unique talent in one subject may make that pace seem too slow for him, while the pace of subjects that pose a challenge to his aptitude may seem too fast. So the mass-production design ends up making him slow down in the former and labour under pressure with the latter to come to the median of 'average'.

What is the purpose of learning? Is it to develop and help realize each person's uniqueness and true potential? If so, how does our education system where rote memorization gets the grades, fulfil it? Only a small aspect of the intellect— memory—is being engaged and sharpened by our education system. Where is the sharpening of thinking, figuring out, developing an opinion, a standpoint that is unique to an individual? Where is the involvement of curiosity, creativity and imagination?

As it is, the role of memory is getting marginalized in the age of Google. Why cram our brains with information that is at our fingertips on the keyboard? But our education system is largely 'informative' as opposed to 'stimulating'. Lessons are *delivered* rather than discussed in a participative format. All you have to do is cram all that information, spill it out verbatim while writing your papers and you're done. The student is not engaged with his material as a result he does not really connect with his subject. Education must involve the student's thinking faculty not just his retentive power. Retention will happen automatically when the classroom is made experiential—through a discussion, debate or such like. Education must help a student develop a viewpoint all his own. That is what sets him apart, develops his uniqueness, his individuality.

The job of education is to reveal our gifts and talents, to enable us to live a joyous life that stems from an understanding of our inner world—not to pitch us against the outer world.

And we're seeing a higher level of consciousness and many more opportunities for people to challenge their present ways of thinking and move into a grander and larger experience of who they really are.

—Neale Donald Walsch

# Where Truth Resides

The Garden of Eden was about innocence; the earthly realm is about knowledge and the heavenly realm is about Truth.

After Adam and Eve partook of the fruit from the tree of knowledge, God had to expel them from Eden and send them to the earth. Now, man could not go back to Eden because innocence was lost, so the only way to salvation was for man to find the Truth and go to heaven.

God wanted man to find the Truth but he wanted to make it difficult, because He knew that post-knowledge man would love challenge and would value things in direct proportion to how unattainable they were. So in order to make the search for Truth the most worthwhile goal, he had to make it hard to attain.

"Where shall I hide it" He thought, "where man is least likely to look?"

He thought of placing it on the highest mountain peak, "But with knowledge man will soon invent all kinds of gizmos and it won't be long before scaling mountain peaks will be only too easy." He thought.

He then thought of hiding it on the bed of the deepest ocean, but knew that even that would soon become accessible to man.

"Where will man never look?" He wondered and wondered. Then suddenly He had a big eureka, "aha!" He said to Himself, "They don't call me God for nothing—what a brilliant idea! I've thought up the one place man will never ever think to look!"

And God hid Truth inside man.

## Insight

1. Enlightenment is no secret.
2. It is not a treasure hunt set up for us by the forces that be, to keep us meaningfully engaged through the span of our lives.
3. There is nothing elusive or esoteric about it.
4. Nor is it an exalted goal that all of humanity must strive for.
5. It is simply our natural state of being and therefore something we can never lose.
6. It is that which we are, when we are not trying to become that which we are not.
7. I'll say that again, it is that which we are, when we are not trying to become that which we are not.
8. But the mind, used as it is to complicating, looks for deeper and hidden meanings.
9. It has been conditioned into believing that anything worthwhile cannot be simple—and definitely not easily available.
10. To *seek* enlightenment is to miss the point.

11. To toil and strive for it, to practice this or that discipline, to feel the need to deserve it are conditioned responses.
12. In fact, enlightenment, liberation, fulfilment, freedom, oneness—whatever name you want to call it by, is effortless, immediate, instantaneous and constantly with us.
13. It is available through a mere shift in perspective.
14. The very strife that we hope to attain it by is in its way.
15. The only purpose effortful-ness ever serves is that it will tire you out such that you give up out of sheer frustration; and in that moment of giving up, what you seek becomes manifest.

# The Design of Consciousness

Awakening is the realization that I have been asleep. It is the beginning of the journey from unconsciousness to enlightenment. Enlightenment is full consciousness. We have often heard it said that the human brain works only at a tenth of its capacity and that the quantum of the unconscious mind is far, far greater than that of the conscious mind. 'Tripping' or the use of stimulants enhances our mind capacity only marginally—and the results are dramatic—creative insights, spiritual highs and even ecstasy. Imagine a state of full consciousness—a state where the whole of the unconscious mind becomes conscious. That is enlightenment—where even the darkest recesses of the mind come under the light of consciousness. It is liberation from the hidden drivers in our mental-emotional makeup which manifest as the tyrannical little voice in the head that dictates our actions in unintended ways. The unconscious mind contains memories of past experiences fused together with certain emotional responses such that they become inseparable. Anything that is even vaguely reminiscent of the experience then becomes the trigger for the same emotional reaction even though the two events may be vastly different. These play out as recurrent emotional patterns in our life. One can be said to be enlightened when these and other such machinations of this unpredictable aspect of the mind are seen clearly in full consciousness. One then has a God-like mastery over life with crystal clarity about its course. Once unconsciousness is dispelled, everything comes under the light of consciousness. That is what enlightenment actually is—not some thunder and lightning phenomenon that leaves in its wake a halo around our heads. When everything in our mind is brought under the light of our 'seeing' or consciousness, we can call ourselves enlightened. Hidden drivers no longer run our lives, making us act helplessly against our own will. It is these drivers that are at the source of all wrongdoings, and in the extreme cases, all crime. For, there is no right or wrong; good or bad—there is only conscious and unconscious. When you act from full consciousness, then whatever action you take, is exactly as it should be.

An evolutionary mutation of consciousness is just round the corner. In the history of evolution, whenever a critical mass of members of a species adapts to a new way of being, mutation happens and the species evolves. A new level of human consciousness is on the verge of emerging. It is just waiting for the critical-mass tipping point. There must have been a period, just before we became full-fledged homo-erectus, when some of us were still using our forelegs for walking while others were using these as hands with increasing dexterity and perhaps already walking on twos. And then suddenly, a critical mass was reached and everyone started following the new model. Thereafter, mutated offspring were born with erect walk and dexterity already programmed into their DNA. Likewise, today we find a host of individuals struggling with challenges of unconsciousness—uncovering the games we play, the masks we hide behind, the multiple identities of ego we live from. As soon as enough of us become consciousness-conscious, that critical mass will be achieved and a new chapter in the story of evolution will begin.

What will that new realm look like? The world will no longer be black and white; good and bad, because at the source of all duality is conscious and unconscious. We paid a huge psychological price for our transition from the animal to civilized state. The process of socialization demanded rigorous discipline, and discipline implies repression of spontaneity. Individuals needed to fit into social moulds—the price was individuality. That individuality—our singular uniqueness—is actually what we call our spirit. The spirit of the individual got alienated. In the larger interest of community building we stopped heeding to it. Over time, this inner voice became more and more feeble. In the new age spirituality, human beings are getting back in touch with this spirit. We had left it behind in the march-past to our scientific glory, where being in step was of supreme importance. We are beginning to listen to it, to reclaim it once again.

Consciousness pioneers and the science of psychology are enabling us to retrieve this lost essence of our selves. So many self awareness businesses, new age groups and organizations, authors and individuals are playing midwife to a new age of consciousness. We are fast approaching the critical mass. The toil and effort of understanding and experiencing this new realm of consciousness will soon cease. We will not need to struggle with it anymore. It is in the air and it is infectious. Everyone will catch it willy-nilly because it is in the natural flow of human evolution.

# Travel Light

In an isolated monastery lived two monks who were great friends as well as spiritual companions. Begging for alms is a spiritual exercise that every monk needs to undertake to kill his ego. Every morning the two would set out together to beg for alms in the village across the river. One morning, it was pouring in sheets as they left for the village. All day it rained incessantly while the monks roamed the village streets. In the evening, on their way back when they reached the river it was in full spate. The two were about to swim back when they noticed a woman hesitating by the banks of the river. One of the monks promptly offered to carry the woman across on his back.

When they got to the other side, the Good Samaritan put the woman safely down and the two monks started walking towards the monastery. They walked on and on. Finally the other monk could hold back no longer.

"Brother," he said, "don't you know we're not supposed to do what you did. Why did you carry that woman on your back?"

"Brother," replied the Good Samaritan, "I put her down a long time ago. Are you still carrying her?"

# Insight

1. Karma is not always an action—a thought that sticks and leaves a residue getting added to our mental baggage is also karma
2. The action performed was not the karma in this case; the thought and interpretation of the action by the second monk was.